Lip Hopping

with the

Fundi-Fu

Poems

SOUTHWARK LIBRARIES

SK 2318826 X

First published in Great Britain in 2010
by Caboodle Books Ltd
Copyright © Adisa 2010

All rights reserved. Apart from any use permitted under UK
copyright law, this publication may only be reproduced,
stored or transmitted, in any form, or by any means with
prior permission in writing from the publishers or in the case
of reprographic production in accordance with the terms
of licences issued by the Copyright Licensing Agency
and may not be otherwise circulated in any form
of binding or cover other
than that in which it is published and without a
similar condition being imposed on
the subsequent purchaser.

A Catalogue record for this book is available
from the British Library.

ISBN 978 0 9565 239 21

Cover Illustration by Mark Stanley
Page Layout by Highlight Type Bureau Ltd
Printed by Cox and Wyman

The paper and board used in the paperback by
Caboodle Books Ltd are natural recyclable products
made from wood grown in sustainable forests.
The manufacturing processes conform to the environmental
regulations of the country of origin.

Caboodle Books Ltd
Riversdale, 8 Rivock Avenue, Steeton, BD20 6SA
www.authorsabroad.com

Dedication:

I would like to thank:

Mummy for the words,

Daddy for the Music,

Ngozi Stephen-Ezeocha for the love

Oluchi & Chike for the inspiration.

London Borough of Southwark

J

SK 2318826 X	
Askews & Holts	08-Feb-2013
821 ADI	£5.99

Introduction

We entered this world and cried that was our first poem.
It was a giant multitasking metaphor full of imagery, colour and texture.

Poetry is pure spirit invisible to the human eye our quest is to make spirit tangible. We achieve this by dressing the spirit in fine cloth called WORDS.

A poem has a resonance that shatters the window of limitation, allowing the writer to walk barefoot in the garden of adventure. Each step we walk on this path illuminates a deeper awareness of self, and the world in which we live.

I believe poetry should be read, sung, and rapped from every corner of the globe, and performed on every stage that can sustain the weight of the spoken word.

Lip Hopping with the Fundi-FU is a collection of poems that were born on the page, but live out their lives on the world stage.

Lip hopping is the art of speaking and performing, Fundi is a Swahili word which means expert, Fu derives form the Chinese Kung-Fu and translates to hard work.

I believe with hard work and application we can all become the Fundi-Fu.

Contents

Lip Hopping with the Fundi-Fu

Bow!
To the power of the Fundi-fu
my broad sword pen cuts through
paper weight MCs
who dare to test my title.
I'll have you in creases like origami
as you fall like a bungee jumper
in the middle of my recital.

I'm Bruce Lee with my one-inch rhyme
and my alliteration nunchaku sticks.
Crushing enemies against the margin
with my acrostic side kicks.

I'll deliver a couplet of jabs
before you've raised your fist.
The Fundi-Fu laughs in your face
with a roundhouse limerick.

I'll infect you with a virus
with my ninja dust haiku.
You'll be sadder than an elegy
screaming out Achoo!

My forms are free flowing verse
you're a list poem with one idea.
I'm a ballad a living legend
you're an epic full of fear.

I'm stealth in my metre
hiding signatures in Urdu Ghazal's.
Camouflaged in metaphor
every syllable yells rebel!

Biff! Bang! Wallop!
My Onomatopoeia has knocked you for six
Now you hide behind personification
Like a magician who's run out of tricks

Many have challenged the Fundi-Fu
millions of Epitaphs bear their name.
I'm the Lip Hop grand master
All hail the king , is your only refrain.

Fundi is a Swahili word for expert.
Fu derives from the word Kung-Fu: it means to work hard
at something.

OO7

Like a secret agent
defending the honour of the spoken word
on a mission to seek out probe and disturb.
The Verbalizer loaded and licensed to kill
stereotypes, hypocrisy, misconceptions
stained on sheets of propaganda
passing as journalistic skill.
In this assassination
truth is the only blood that spills.

Close encounters of the classroom kind

My teacher's an alien
His head revolves three hundred and sixty degrees.
He hears me talking under my breath
he says, "Bless you." before I sneeze.

I know he's not human
He has no lips his beard is so thick.
He eats the school lunch
and he's never had a day off sick.

He can count to hundred
Just using the fingers on his hands.
He writes backwards on the blackboard
Only the class gerbil understands.

Beneath the bike sheds
Is where he hides his space ship.
I've seen smoke clouds rising
I bet the playground is the landing strip.

I think Ms. Butler knows the truth
for some strange reason she's too shy to say.
Maybe that's why I heard giggles
in the stock cupboard during wet play.

I'm going to tell the Head
that my teacher is not from this planet.
But if Sir found out it was me
he'd turn me into a statue of granite.

I've got to be brave
Remember Will Smith Men in Black.
Dark shades, black suit
and my inhaler in case of an asthma attack.

It's four thirty the school is empty
my teacher is working late in his room.
I creep up behind him draw my inhaler and squeeze!
There's an almighty KABOOM!

"Its half past eight you're going to be late for school"

Dad raps his fist on my bedroom door.
I jump up so high I hit my head on the ceiling
then collapse in a heap on the floor.

Maybe my teacher's not an alien after all.

Bungee jump hill

Jack and Jill bungee jumped off the hill

for they wanted some time alone.

The rope snapped, Jill broke her back

and Jack laughed all the way home.

A True Pearl

Mango textured skin
a seed of love
planted deep within her heart.
Trundling through life's market place
not too slow, never too fast.
Old fashioned some say
just like the horse and cart.

A silent cottage
with her back to the wind.
Like a willow in autumn
words of wisdom
fall from her lips.
She got Jazz in her body
keeping perfect time
to the rhythm of her hips.

Working harder than a beaver
two mothers' loads
balanced on her head.
She's black carbon
many cannot see her light,
beneath her onyx skin
I see a diamond shining bright.

Wonderful world

Ever wondered where rainbows go
when the rain and sun have called a truce.
Ever wondered why elders say
"things were so much better in my youth"

Ever wondered why parents talk in riddles,
then say "am I making myself clear."
Ever wondered how a simple onion
can make a grown man shed a tear.

Ever wondered why wars are started
with the intention to bring peace.
Ever wondered how computers
eat kilobytes yet they have no teeth.

Ever wondered why common sense
is called common, when it's not.
Ever wondered why a sentence
is naked without a full stop.

Ever wondered why the giant thunder
with all its power never shows its face.
Ever wondered what the world would be like
if we all believed in the human race.

Ever wondered why we value gold
yet disrespect her mother, Earth.
Ever wondered why love is so scarce
when every child had a sack full at birth.

Ever wondered why pianos have keys
but can't open any locks.
Ever wondered why books have spines
and three hands are pinned to a clock.

Ever wondered why children want to be older
and the adults want to be young.
Ever wondered how words and rhythm
can take a bad situation and turn it into fun.

Ever wondered do poets have the answers
to the many questions they ask.
Ever thought am I who I say I am
or am I just wearing a mask.

*If you answered yes to any of the above
Then maybe you're a poet too.*

Acrostic Poetry

P ure rays of light
O pening
E nvelopes of potential
T rapped inside the
R ecess of
Y our mind!

Don't hold your tongue

Their mothers spoke

Amharic

Urdu

Cantonese

Bengali

Albanian

Igbo

Swahili

and Twee.

Their mothers spoke

Hausa

Spanish

Celtic

Gujarati

Russian

Dutch

Fula

and Somali.

Their mothers spoke

Romanian

Portuguese

Patio

Sanskrit

English

Creole

Xhosa

and Arabic.

Many mothers

one human tongue.

Forbidden fruit

My number muncher

My alphabet piano

My finger sofa

My Dr Who's passport

My pixel Picasso

My binary jukebox

My alloy star gate

My 3D theatre

My document hoarder

My inkless press

My sleepless worker

My blue tooth sniffer

My edible apple

You're so morish

I could eat you with one bite.

Gap the Mind
Mind the Gap

Gather like emperor penguins
make no effort to move inside the train.
Try to board just as the doors are closing.
This should cause delay.
Travel well past your ticket zone
then tell the inspector I have no means to pay.

Make no eye contact
in the event this happens
look away and pretend to laugh.
Turn your not so personal stereo
up to eleven and let those speakers blast.

Occupy the whole of the armrest
invade the enemy's space.
Dig your elbow in their ribcage
sneeze loudly
without covering your face.

Crack open this morning's breakfast
two slices of marmite and a hard boiled egg.
Read your neighbour's newspaper
trying your best not to move your head.

If they read slowly
offer to turn the page.
Expect resistance
some folks just don't know
how to control their tube-rage.

Gumboot Diamonds

There is a sound
that lives 300 feet beneath
the surface of despair.
Where dreams once danced
like cart-wheeling children
cutting through the yellow air.

Men stomp with bronze feet
kicking the listener back to life
with a rhythm heavy like death.
Crossing language borders
resurrection in their eyes
and freedom on their breath.

Clawing diamonds from rocks
for a moment they're rich.
Finders are not keepers
in this apartheid opera.
So when the sun dies
there is no meat on their dish.

Now rubber and hand
play Satchmo blues.
Words become weapons
aimed at greedy boys
who call themselves men.

Cracks!
and slaps!
Cascade over rocky brows
serenading distant wives.
Cooling the sting
Of this underground oven
where hope is cooked alive.

There is a sound
older than words
a symphony of war and play.
When the ngoma starts
in this underground theatre
thunder turns and runs away.

Hats don't keep my head warm

Hats don't keep my head warm
they have more important work to do.
My hat is a house of magic
but there are no white rabbits in view.

So much more than a ball of wool
or cotton moulded in a circular shape.
When I don my hat I can fly
and I don't need Superman's cape.

I walk in the tradition of the hat men
my father was a hat man too.
He had hats for cricket, dominoes,
playing steel pan and even sitting on the ....bus

His hats had presence and style
even the ones that stunk of old spice.
When walking down the road
Dad made the wind look twice.

Hats are like masks
allowing the wearer to disappear.
Presenting a wall of confidence
built with the cement of fear.

Hats are time machines
you can skinny dip in the fountain of youth.
Direct your own west end musical
starring fantasy as the hero, with his sidekick truth.

Beneath the royal crown
the owner reigns supreme.
A hat is more than a hat
just like a wish is more than a dream.

Barbershop blues

I say a silent prayer

the barber prepares for the deathblow.

His weapon falls like a guillotine

every follicle on my head screams No!

My hair did not ask to die

this humble servant of mine.

It's judgement day the jury's in

being a loyal tenant his only crime

The barbershop becomes an abattoir

sterile razors, scissors and clippers

dripping with the blood of oil.

Tiny curls belly flop to the ground

their dying words fall like kings

stranded like seeds on barren soil.

As they sing the barbershop blues

1st Love

Like snow without white
like a story with no end.
Like Jazz without Dizzy
like a spring with no bend.

Like algebra without maths
like a tree with no roots.
Like a kite without the wind
like an orchard with no fruits.

Like an alphabet without letters
like a river with no bed.
Like a rapper without a mic
like a bullfight with no red.

You left me alone.

Dizzy refers to **Dizzy Gillespie** the African American Jazz musician
who created Be-bop.

The Flour Power Poet

There's a poet visiting our school
I've seen his poster in the library,
Eyes larger than golf balls
A neck longer than a bassoon.
My teacher says, "His words are full of power"
I think Poets are boring like plain flour.

He came through the school gate
Running like an ostrich, and ten minutes late
An old leather bag tucked under his arm
Sweating like a leaky tap, trying to keep calm.
My teacher says, "His words are full of power"
Poets are boring like plain flower.

He shook hands with the Head
then slower than a sloth began to tread
into the hall, to meet the restless crowd.
My teacher said," The poet will read for an hour"
We chorused, "Poetry is boring like plain flour"

He read a poem about fleas,
Talked of flowers blowing in the breeze
He rhymed orange with porridge
Read Shakespeare in slang
He began every sentence with "Yo Man!"

We were tiger cubs with sharp claws
Our snarls turned the poets milk sour.
He squeaked, " What do you think of the show so far?"
We shouted!
"Poetry is boring like plain flour"

He tried everything
Alliteration, personification
Haiku and Rhyming,
Waving his arms like a conductor.
But he looked like a monkey climbing
His way up a very sticky gum tree
With his pink bum exposed for the whole school to see.

Like a defeated boxer
He slumped into the wooden chair
Opened his satchel, pulled out a poem
And his soul he started to bear.

He didn't ask the audience to be quiet
Or stop flicking blue-tack in his face.
He told us a story about a bully
Who answered to the name of Mace.

When Mace was in year seven
He found maths hard, and science boring.
Girls never laughed at his jokes
In the back of the history class, Mace was snoring.

I was transfixed
I almost forgot how to breathe
The poet spun words like a tailor
I became the thread in his weave.

The bully in his poem
Didn't share my birthday
He 'd never visited my street
His mother wasn't called Irene
But I was convinced the poet was talking about ME!

I listened like a mother searching for her child
beneath the rubble of an earthquake,
he turned my world into an ice rink
I was skidding into the barriers I couldn't find the brake.

The poet seemed to suggest he understood
the language the bully uses in order to be heard
Muscles and razor sharp fists
are the only options when they run out of words.

It all stopped
The day his teacher said
"That's a good poem Mace
Do you have any more?"

He no longer needed to bully others
He could take it out on the page
With a right hook and a uppercut
His knockout poems would soothe his rage

Today, Mace reads poetry worldwide
Opening minds like a spring flower
My teacher was right
His words are full of power.

I've changed my mantra
Poetry isn't boring it's amazing
But I still compare it to flour
But now it's self-raising!

Headteacher

Head off the notion to be too head strong.
Headhunters' baskets are full of heads
Who did not heed this song.
Headless people walk in circles
unaware, these panicking chickens are already dead.
Baskets full of aching heads,
worrying over what's been done and said.
Head teacher is your guide to success
if you're willing to be led.
You see!
The real head teacher dwells in the place you call your Head.

I'm on the Menu

His smile a hot water bottle
defrosting human hearts
bound in the cold rhythm
of another day.

His speech
a runaway saxophone
On a brass train track
Man!
He got so much to say.

His touch
morish like jollof rice
his fingers wrap like vines.
I'm lost in this human maze
and I can't read the signs.

His ebony eyes
precise like lasers
as they burn into my soul.
I'm dessert
for this baby python
who swallows me whole.

My Instrument my pen

My instrument my pen
a steel quill tied to a hunter's spear.
Black blood squirts
through bamboo veins
leaving tattoos on the papyrus
of your soul.

My instrument my pen
ebony drumsticks
beating
Afro-beat blues
of
Redemption song
on racism's taut goatskin
head.

My instrument my pen
scribing Maat Laws
but they aren't new
they surfaced before
like African Moors
guided by Yemanja
arriving on European shores.

My instrument my pen
daubing murals of inspiration
on red, black and green landscapes.
Refocusing your image of my nation
shattering windowpanes
of mental procrastination.

My instrument my pen
engraving future footprints
on our children's beach.
Dousing flames of fear
Ignorance and deceit.
Dunking metaphors of love
into plain paper baskets
like wings were attached to my feet.

My instrument my pen
rapping griot tales
Round full moon fires
re-kindling the ancestors
unifying our voices
in celebration choirs.

*In Yoruba mythology Yemanja is the female deity that represents
the ocean, the essence of motherhood, and the protector of children.*

*Maat: the Ancient Egyptian Goddess of truth, balance, order, law,
morality, and justice.*

*Griot: is a West African poet, praise singer, and wandering musician,
considered a repository of oral tradition*

Boot Crazy

My boots have been with me
for the longest of time.
Every day they mature
like a vintage red wine.

As they get older
the better they look.
My boots have fallen
head over heels in love with my foot.

I polish them daily
and they always look smart
no matter how hard I try
I can't keep them apart.

My boots have been with me
through the good and the bad.
They make me feel happy
and comfort me when I am sad.

My boots protect me like a warrior
with a shield and a spear.
Leading from the front
chest raised high immune to fear.

But there's one thing about my boots
that I don't like and this I must confess.
It's when my boots decide
to step in a big pile of fresh dog's mess.

But when I take them off at night
and lay my head to rest.
I can't help but think
my black boots are the best.

Future Masterpiece

If we could paint the future
and hang it in a frame.
From that moment onwards
the world would never be the same.

We would recycle paper
and turn it back into trees.
Turn honey into pollen
and feed it to the bees.

We'd throw war out the window
and watch it shatter on the floor.
Prize open the door of understanding
hypnotize the rich to give to the poor.

There'd be a children's parliament
we'd sit and discuss issues of the day.
Adults who refused to listen
would be kept in during play.

If we could paint the future
and hang it in a frame.
From that moment onwards
the world would never be the same.

The earth would be seen as sacred
the rain forest a holy shrine.
Caretakers for a season
no one could say,
"that piece of land is mine."

We'd invent new ways of travelling
flying cars, that ran on fresh air.
We'd have robots to do the cleaning
we'd call them Bush-extractor and grizzly-Blair.

Racism would dissolve like snow
when zapped by truth rays from the sun.
Martin Luther King's dream would be complete
when there's respect for everyone.

If we could paint the future
and hang it in a frame.
From that moment onwards
the world would never be the same.

We humans would create a new religion
we'd call it giving back so we can live.
Its focus would not be receiving
it would be based on what you can give.

The future is a present
Unwrapped in a different time
Swaddled in the past
the future is yours and mine.

If we could paint the future
and hang it in a frame.
From that moment onwards
the world would never be the same.

Jack's sensitive tummy

Jack Sprat could eat no curry.
His wife could eat no rice.
So between them both
they ate Chinese.

Sweetbread Communion

Friday night was sweetbread night
I'd hear whistling from the kitchen
a sign dad was about to bake bread
It was always the same tune.
(Oh island in the sun)

He'd roll back his sleeves
as if folding the St Vincent flag.
He preferred fresh yeast
huge hands breaking wet clay.

Balancing on a wooden stool
 I'd watch his problems dissolve.
The marriage of yeast and sugar
turned the kitchen into a brewery.

When he sure no one was looking
he'd add the secret ingredient
fresh grated coconut, then stir
until the sweet splinters disappeared.

Next, the flour made its entrance
from the lofty height of the sieve.
Dad's arms resembled a concrete mixer
With his mechanical gyrating.

His tennis ball biceps
expanding and contracting.
The mixture slides like a sledge
on the snow white flour.

Into the deep tins to sleep
a damp tea towel for a blanket.
As they snore they rise
their pop bellies facing the sun.

Dad opens the furnace to be greeted by
golden faces with raisins for eyes.
Pressing two fingers into their foreheads
they bounce back like mini trampolines.

A sponge dipped in nutmeg and honey water
Christens the newborn bread.

(Oh island in the sun)

Just 10

Three months in no man's land
barbed wire words cloud his sky.
They denied him three times
only the Creator heard his cry.

Placing a crown of mockery like a halo
above this Nigerian prince's head.
Drunkard hyenas gather
watching his city crumble
licking his tears as he bled.

"Just wait till tomorrow"
"Just pay them no mind"
"Just fight back"
"Just trust in the Lord the answer he will find."

Just 10 seconds
for Peckham's
shooting star
to fall from grace
into cold concrete.

They severed the artery of our future
now flowers clothe the silent street.
Just 10 years old.
Just 10 steps from home.
A boy called Damilola Taylor sleeps.

Mama Always Told Me

Mama Always Told Me

Son walk the streets with your head held high
you have no limitations if you want to you can fly.
Success does not come to those who sit down and wait
if you don't knock no one will open the gate.

Mama Always Told Me

Put God first in everything you do
believe in yourself and your dreams will come true.
Some will try to hold you down
never regret your skin is brown.

Mama Always Told Me

The road of life is rough and oh so long
when you fall down pick yourself up and carry on.
Respect your parents and elders so your days may be long
when you have children of your own, sing to them this song.

Mama Always Told Me

If you play with puppy, one day dawg lick ya mouth.
No matter how hard the problem you can work it out.

Mama Always Told Me

Put a little by for a rainy day
remember what you sow shall be your pay.
There's a time to work and a time to play
bend the tree while it's young, so when it's older it won't go astray.

Mama Always Told Me

When turkey foot bruk it keep company with fowl
try to see everything around you just like the owl.

Mama Always Told Me

You'll never miss the water till the well runs dry
and just because you're a man
it doesn't mean you can't cry.
In the classroom of life
don't be afraid to pose the question WHY!
There's no such thing as failure
as long as you make up your mind to try.

Mama Always Told Me

A child who doesn't heed their mother
will have to drink pepper, lime juice and salt.
You will not be judged by your words
but by the content of your heart.

My Ridley market

Grown men howl like wolves on heat.
Mountains of citrus piled to the sky.
Snake charmers air their wares
as a black goddess walks by.

Salt fish and mackerel
fight for air supremacy
children barricade their nose.
Dad ducks into the record shop
a chance for mum to buy more clothes.

Pushing and shoving
a new Olympic sport
elbows cocked, and ready to fight.
These E8 gladiators
exchange blows till the price is right.

Four by four shopping baskets
taxi down the runway
experiencing turbulence
as ankles and feet become their prey.

Dalston models on tarmac catwalk.
Bodies wrapped in cling film jeans.
Heads rock inside portable nightclubs
as reggae and soca leaks through the seams

Mother tongues colour the canvas.
Human potential seasons the air.
These voices of culture and tradition
bear witness to Hackney's flare.

Mobile Mania

I want a mobile phone
but I don't know why
all my mates have got one
So why can't I

I sit like a sack of iron filings
commercials draw me to the magnetic screen .
"Hey Mum I want one of those".
Mum says, " I don't have money to buy phone".
I just think she's being mean.

I told her!
"Everybody who's anybody
Got one welded to their hand
Nokia, Apple, Blackberry
It don't matter the brand."

It's got to have removable faces
to co-ordinate with my Versace jeans
Illuminated keypad so I can see it in the dark
a vibrating battery cause,
I just like the sensation.

I want a mobile phone
but I don't know why
all my mates have got one
So why can't I

I heard the radio jingle
a talk plan to make you the envy of your friends
top up tokens pay as you go
free evenings and free weekends.

I want one with the latest games and gadgets
a flip down lid like the one Nio sports in The Matrix
a large screen so I can send images & text.

It's got to be GPS friendly,
even though I am not quite sure what GPS means.
Ring tones with a thousand themes
from all the baddest movies
including Oliver yeah you know that scene
where Artful Dodger sings
"I'll do anything for you dear, anything".

I want a mobile phone
but I don't know why
all my mates have got one
So why can't I?

My teacher tried to fool me the other day
he said, "radiation from phones can warm up your brain"
Damn! He must think gullible is my middle name.

I want a mobile phone
but I don't know why
all my mates have got one
So why can't I

If I had a mobile phone
I'd defend it with my life.
These days guys will jack your phone
at the drop of a hat
and not think twice.

But if they tried to jack my phone
I'd get vexed like David Banner.
My shirt would stretch and tear
jeans come apart at the seams.

I'd beat them so badly
Like Michael J Fox
they'd want to go back in time
and turn this whole episode into a dream.

I want a mobile phone
but I don't know why
all my mates have got one
So why can't I

Everyone's going mobile everyone except me
this makes me weird different from the rest
If I had a mobile phone
Donna Smith would be so impressed.

Mum bought me an iphone for my birthday
I can watch movies, browse the web and edit
But there's just one problem
I can't phone my friends, cause I got no credit.

DJ Cat and the moonwalk rat

Hey diddle diddle
the cat scratches on the turntable
the rat jumped into the moon
thinking it was cheese, took an almighty bite
the big hairy spider was full of fright
and the mummy ran away with its tomb.

Lady Onyx

Kind enough to house the baby
She's the washing line that holds the stars.
The gold that runs through nature's veins
she's the power in the diplomat's cars.

She's the belt of respect
that ties the martial art suit.
She's the centre of the earth
home for the baobab tree roots.

She's the financial caviar
for a wealthy diet.
She's the Tardis inside our heads
when the curtain falls and all is quiet.

She's the solar eclipse
many wait a lifetime to see.
She's a runaway stallion
leaving no footprints on her quest to be free.

She's the coffee in my cup
no need for white clothes.
Like an uncut diamond
she dresses in carbon robes.

She's the view inside the cocoon
before the butterfly takes flight.
She's the backdrop to life's movie
as the credits scroll into the night.

She's a natty dread hairstyle
that unites the people like rope.
She's an Old Man River spiritual
her voice brings ten tons of hope.

She's limitless like the desert
more attractive than quicksand in space.
Behind her back many mock her
too afraid to say it to her face.

She is the absorber of light
Lady Onyx with a shine.
She's the stereotyped refugee
she's the new black
and she's mine.

What is Poetry?

Poetry is everywhere
Poetry is music to my ear
Poetry is a graceful dancer with elegance and flair
Poetry has many shapes and forms but poetry is not square
Poetry is written on paper but poetry doesn't live there
For poetry is in your eyes in your smile and even in your tears

Poetry is in the way you walk
Some folks walk around as if they're barmy
Some folks walk like they're in the army
Some people walk as slow as a snail
Some people walk like they have four legs and a tail

Poetry is an African drum playing a heartbeat
Poetry is the cold wind that blows, and the sun that gives us heat
Poetry is dad's old boots and dad's cheesy feet
Poetry wakes me in the morning and closes my eyes at night to sleep
Poetry is a plate of fresh vegetables because I don't eat meat

Poetry is a rhythm that goes on and on and on
Poetry is Bob Marley singing my favorite song

"Buffalo soldier dreadlock Rasta"

Poetry lives and poetry cannot die
Poetry is my imagination
If I want to I can touch the sky
Poetry is the sound of a newborn baby
when it begins to cry
Mamma!
Poetry needs to be read like a bird needs to fly
So when I ask the question
 "What is poetry?"
You should all be very clear
Because,
"Poetry is everywhere".

Who is Jasper Dash?

Who is Jasper Dash?
This invisible prophet
Etching parables on the city's face
Spitting 3d rainbows
To an aerosol rhythm
Fusing religion, politics and race.

2000 years of wisdom
Crammed into a seventeen year old frame
Knowledge is power to many
But to some knowledge equals pain.

Now he don't know where it came from
He can't tell a soul he's some sort of sage
So when the moon is king, he dons his cloak
And on the canvas of life paints another page.

Pouncing from park bench to roof top
like an urban tiger gripping his tin
his collages become lifejackets
for those who have forgotten how to swim.

Who is Jasper Dash?
This invisible prophet
Etching parables on the city's face
Spitting 3d rainbows
To an aerosol rhythm
Fusing religion, politics and race

He's the lighthouse that's too bright
Warning people of the tsunami to come
Executing corruption at dawn
Freedom bullets through an aerosol gun.

A superhero dwells beneath the Reebok hood
the world sees a criminal, another lost youth
from the college of reality a straight A-student
Jasper dash is on a mission to reveal the truth.

Fumes circle then lick the city skyline
he exhales as wet paint cries on a concrete wall
and just for a moment, the invisible man
from a SE10 street is now ten feet tall.

Who is Jasper Dash?
This invisible prophet
Etching parables on the city's face
Spitting 3d rainbows
To an aerosol rhythm
Fusing religion, politics and race

Jasper squashes beef before it happens
a natural leader he follows no gang
armed to the teeth with vocabulary
never afraid to make a stand.

This teenage councillor
always strapped with a book.
He spits rhymes of reason
That makes the blind open their eyes and look.

Jasper Dash needs no soapbox
to bring the community together.
He's the neighbour hood watch
under his Lip-hop umbrella.

More skills than Ronaldo
when tackling crime on his beat
This under cover artist
a guardian angel of the street

When Jasper speaks the world is deaf
family and friends can't quite make him out
but with a dash or blue and a dash of red
the silent warrior begins to shout.

His art is loved by the masses
vilified and ridiculed by a few
street politics without the spin
from a young mans point of view.

Jasper lives by his motto
I am the word, and the word is we.
Expression is fundamental
and graffiti is the passport to be free.

Phat Bucks

A man with skinny legs

walked into a skinny shop

ordered a skinny cappuccino

and a skinny chocolate chip muffin to go.

The skinny waitress said "that will be a fiver."

He pulled his skinny wallet from his pocket

paid the waitress with a skinny smile

She took the money and placed it in the phat till.

Words

Words are foods that cannot be eaten but still they feed my mind
Wallow in the words of wisdom and you'll be surprised by what you
   find
Words together make a sentence a sentence makes a paragraph
Some words make me real angry and some words make me laugh
Words are used to hypnotize and put some folks in a trance
Words entwined with rhythm and music can make me want to dance

Words exchanged between two people if misunderstood could make
   them fight
Words used like a key in a lock could expose you to the light
Words speak of different cultures their success and their plight
Words can be real inspiring like when Bob Marley took the mic

Some people say "I want to be rich. Without money life's a bore".
But let me say the more you know of life the more you feel secure
Words can help you understand the future and what's gone on before
See the book as a stairway leading to a door
Once inside keep searching till you reach the core
And if you get lost I'll find your message washed up on the shore

Inside you is a story just waiting to take flight
What I am really trying to say is every one of us can write
Write of wars, hatred and the peace that is yet to come
Write of people understanding the tongue must replace the gun
Write of nature to which we all belong

Write of living for today for tomorrow you could be gone
But if you leave words in a book your legacy will carry on
And maybe your words will inspire the next generation
To learn from you and go deeper and then go beyond
So get a pen and some paper sit right down and make a start
No need to worry about the format
   as long as it comes from the heart.

My Teddy Bear

My teddy bear has dreadlocks
right down to the middle of his back
each spiralling like a corkscrew
Tight springs painted black.

Teeth gleaming like a carpet of snow
marbles dipped in chocolate
make my teddy bear's eyes
with his banana shape mouth
he always looks like he's just had a surprise.

When he sleeps his mouth is always open
like he's trying to catch flies.

Walking slower than a tortoise
but with the bounce of a hare
each stride he takes he shouts!
Somebody stop me if you dare.

My teddy bear jives to jazz
swings his hips to the soul
spins on his head to hip-hop
twists like an acrobat
when he hears rock & roll.

Decked out in kente cloth
like an Ashanti King
robes of red, gold and green
each finger is smothered in a gold ring.

My teddy bear adores his food
especially plantain and rice and peas.
He does cartwheels backwards
for my mums famous macaroni cheese.
Polishing his plate squeaky clean
he lets rip a burp louder than a clap of thunder
as he loudly proclaims excuse me please!

My teddy bear is family
much more than stuffing and fur.
He's like my third brother
when I rub his head he starts to purr.

We can not be separated
for together we are a team.
The funny thing is I can only see him
when I close my eyes to dream.

Africa inside me

She's in the Igbo yam
that graces my plate.
Her scent lingers like shea butter
massaged into my face.

She lubricates my hips
in the Soukous water of Congo.
Steel pan for skis I ride to
Trinidad and Tobago.

She's red bean soup
a Jamaican baseline.
She's the wiggle and roll
of auntie's waistline.

With one almighty push
she bore the blues.
Jazz followed swiftly
bringing good news.

With a chisel in her left
and a hammer in her right,
she carved 7 steps to heaven
Pyramids on earth map the stars at night.

Adinkra cloth ribbons of sunlight
hang on her broad shoulders.
Each thread an alphabet in code
drenched in the red earth of home.

Her voice becomes the talking drum
like Kwame Nkrumah
Serenading the brand new day.
We pay our respects to our ancestors
So they will continue to light the way.

Some call her "Shango" God of thunder
they say "fire and lightning runs through her veins."
She is Maasai afraid of no one
the lion that will never be tamed.

Passing the baton of transformation
From the old to the young.
Recycling ancient wisdom
for nothing is new under the sun.

Resurrecting her heritage
to its rightful place once more.
Africa's hand has touched the world
of this you can be sure.

Night Bandits

Scaling the walls like ninjas
they terrorize my home.
Flashing past my ears like bees
mating with a microphone.

Dressed in black armour
their samurai eyes full of fire
to complete their mission
their one and only desire.

Equipped with P.R.T. (Personal Radar Tracking)
they smell their victim five miles away
it's just a matter of time
before the hunter claims his prey.

They search for crimson treasure
buried beneath my skin
one quick jab
and the siphoning begins.

These guys mean business
and they're not interested in money
to them my blood is a delicacy
and it's Sweeter than honey.

Like camels gorging on water
licking their lips with delight
then as smooth as a helicopter
they disappear into the night.

I play dead, as I track the leader
from the corner of my eye.
This bedroom is not big enough for two of us
tonight one of us will have to die.

I can't believe it

Its doing one-armed push ups on my lamp shade
displaying its acrobatic skill
back arched like a tomcat
I move in for the kill.

Hands held out before me
as if holding a basket ball.
Walking like a zombie
towards the bedroom door.

CLAP!
Got Ya!
It's time to switch off the light.
Game over my friend
there'll be no more biting tonight.

I open my hands
to view the grizzly remains
what was once a brave warrior,
is now a sticky red stain.

What do I do with the body?
Flush it down the toilet
for a burial at sea.
Bury it in the garden
beneath the cherry tree.
Throw it out the window
let its spirit run wild and free.

I say a prayer for the mosquito
Who fought with his heart and not with his head
wash my hands brush my teeth
and climb back into bed.

A marriage made in beef

Humpty Dumpty slept in his nest
trying to catch the midday sun.
When he awoke he was married to a burger
half eaten
inside a sesame seed bun.

Oistin's comedy store

Get your fresh snapper
three dollars a pound
chants the man
with the oily skin.
Throwing his voice like the morning net
as he swiftly reels them in.

Solemn faces file past,
these tiled tombs of slate
pausing then peering deeply
into these sun kissed bodies, lying in state.

"No touching!
What you see is what you get
yes you with the push up mouth
you been feeling up all morning
and you no buy nothing yet."

These rainbow creatures
once king of the deep
look so alive, I wonder
if I yelled run!
Would they awake from their sleep?

Get your fresh snapper
three dollars a pound
chants the man
with the oily skin.
Throwing his voice like the morning net
as he swiftly reels them in.

The crowd swells
like gongo peas soaking in water.
Moving mystically and speaking in tongues
the fisherman is a now a preacher
with wisdom of the local healer.

Trevally goes nice with a little rice and peas.
In Saturday soup, red bream is your fish.
Flying fish with turn cornmeal
Man!
You eating Cou cou!
We national dish.

You can
Steam
Bake
Barbecue
Smoke
or even fry.

Fish can prevent all kind of disease
Trust me!
Eat fish every day
you might get old but you'll never die.

Get your fresh snapper
three dollars a pound
chants the man
with the oily skin.
Throwing his voice like the morning net
as he swiftly reels them in.

I'll take five pound of snapper
give me two of them bream
ten dollars worth of dolphin
three kilo's of jacks
and make sure the whole lot clean.

Miss Lou cracks a joke
"Clean the fish properly
I wear dentures
and can't afford
to get scales stuck in me teeth"
The market becomes a carnival
as the crowd stagger like skittles
in the middle of the street.

Wet dollar bills are exchanged
for blue plastic bags
pregnant with heads and fins.
The tide goes out for another day
at Oistins.

Oistins is a large fish market in Barbados

7 steps ahead

1875
A black star lands
on a busy Croydon street.
A head full of blue notes
and a heart full of beats.

7 winters pass
this musical genius starts to grow.
His nimble fingers articulate perfection
as he grasps the violin bow.

7 years of training
composition occupies his mind.
This master Taylor wove
African American threads
into Sierra Leone designs.
Creating a Black British genre
light years ahead of his time.

Smelting poetry with music
like a modern day Hip-Hop star.
Taylor poured his music
over the words of Paul Lawrence Dunbar.
7 Pan - African romances, celebrate
I am because we are.

Hiawatha's wedding piece
nobody knows the trouble I've seen
elevated his music to worldwide acclaim.
President Theodore Roosevelt requested to meet
the genius behind Hiawatha fame.

1912
A black star returns to heaven.
Samuel Coleridge Taylor
dies at the age of 37.

The man is gone
his name remembered by a few.
His spirit lives in his music
Pan-African and true.

Pins and Needles

Awoken by a sensation of an intruder in my bed
A hand cold as ice and heavy like lead.
What brings this intruder here?
 I don't know.
Fear saturates my body from head to toe.
I scream at the top of my voice "Who are you? Please let go".
Fear turns into tossing and turning
I fall into a heap on the floor.
I've got to get out of this room,
But I can't see the door.
The walk becomes a jog the jog becomes a run
Words try to leave my mouth but I've now become dumb.
If this is someone's idea of a joke this isn't fun.
As my right hand flicked on the light it all became clear
You see my left hand had gone to sleep
And pins and needles was the reason for my fear.

Black Magic

B elittled in dictionaries
L abelled the bringer of doom
A ccused of socialising with evil
C ondemned to a lightless room
K icked to the back of the pile

But I wear my black with a smile.

The Gatekeeper

I am the aboriginal painting
that once spoke of divination
and the journey of a boy becoming a man.
The same painting
gathering dust on a glass shelf
untouched by a human hand.

I am the gatekeeper
on these chess board streets
the pawn that became the king.
Surveying the ocean
from the door of no return
I sing in the key of win.

I am the voice of trees
whose limbs have embraced
dying men who shared the same hue.
I am the scent of sugar and rum
crammed into branded barrels
the misery of many brings joy to a few.

I am the buffalo soldier
who defended mother earth.
When the children tried to
cut out their parent's tongue.

I am the great wall of Zimbabwe
my spine a house of stone.
Needing no media cement
I stand before my final curtain alone.

Seventh Heaven

They crossed the seven seas.
They resisted the seven deadly sins.
They visited the Seven Wonders of the World.
They upheld the seven pillars of wisdom.
They kissed snow white.
They shook hands with the seven dwarfs.
They walked for seven days.
They arrived at seventh heaven.
They were still thirsty for knowledge.
They opened a can of 7-up
then burped seven times.

TAKE TIME!

Take a hexagon of honey from a hive,
on a hazy afternoon.
Take a note from a lullaby
sung to a baby in a womb.

Take a single raindrop,
before it hits the ground.
Take a grain of sand in an oyster
spinning round and round.

Take the pollen from a petal,
all covered in dew.
Take the calm after the storm
as the sun comes breaking through.

Take the striking of a flint,
causing the wood to ignite.
Take the precision of an owl,
severing the air with its prey insight.
Take the second you know you're wrong
but still you say you're right.
Take the exact moment day becomes night.

Take a magic word whispered in your ear,
take the scent of life filling you with fear.
Take the taste of death, trapped inside a tear.
Take a good look at God
as in the mirror you stare.

Take time to see
all these manifestations
as reflections of you and me.

In the Month of my Childhood

In the month of my childhood
Beano was my daily rag
Dennis the Menace was the man.
I wrote to him religiously
to me he was Eminem
I guess I was Stan.

In the month of my childhood
food and I were lovers
Uncle Ben's rice with curry goat meat.
Abseiling into the kitchen, at midnight
I was 007 licensed to EAT.

I escaped through the square window
in the playschool house
solved crimes in the afternoon
with my partner Danger Mouse.

Thomas The Tank Engine
Ran out of steam.
So I recycled rubbish with the Wombles
from Wimbledon Green.

In the month of my childhood
every man, woman and child
wanted the answer to the question
Who shot JR?
and every teenager in the land
wanted to drive Pam Ewing's car.

Seven o'clock every Thursday evening
we camped around the house fire
A three channel Bush TV.
I travelled back in time with Dr. Who
400 years to meet Kunta Kinte.

Those roots wrapped themselves, like pythons
around my fragile mind.
I knew they were actors
sometimes tears are hard to find.

In the month of my childhood
My brother was Russia
and I was the USA.
Our cold war existence
went far beyond child's play.

I called him the black sheep of the family
my ignorance was straight out of Snow White.
He called me a flat nose pig
which always led to a fight.

We were one hundred metre specialists
running away from our culture.
Gaining self worth from the media
like 2 starved vultures.

In the month of my childhood
I played drums in the family band.
We were Luton's answer to the Jackson 5
I found my voice with the drumsticks in my hand.

Dad ran a tight ship as bandleader.
He speciality was mandolin
and when the spirit took over
he'd con the audience into believing he could sing.

Kenroy held the rhythm close,
like a winning hand in poker.
On the double decker keyboard
my brother was no joker.

Keith swayed like a palm tree
whilst plucking the big bad bass.
Sporting his 80's wet look
man he was dripping all over the place.

In the month of my childhood
Friday night discos
St. John's church hall.
the congregation ignites
as the sound head butts the wall.

Baptised by the vocals
I swam in the river of Ska.
Madness were one step beyond
with, "My girls mad at me".
And "I like driving in my car".

Wearing corrugated trilby hats
starched trousers in silver two tone.
This JA/UK Fusion was the ticket
for the boat that carried me home.

In the month of my childhood
2004 was the language of Star Trek
we dreamed of cars that ran on thin air.
Football 24/7 on your screen
Turning 18 and being able to drink beer.

In the month of my childhood
I realised time was a good old friend
who wasn't coming back.

Tangerine Smile

Your smile is golden
a ray of light.
In your presence
my spirit takes flight.

I will capture your smile
and lock it away
and in times of solitude
release your smile
into my day.

Watch Out the sleep train's coming

I lift his body to the stars
and pray for the train
the words "it wont be long now"
drizzle on his head like sweet rain.

I whisper stories of trains packed with dreams
coming to take him away
he just burps, and slaps my face
this is his idea of play.

We do the salsa
from wardrobe to window
like two giant kites,
three steps fast two steps slow.

My voice coaxes sleep
like the snake charmer's flute
enticing this mystical creature
who appears to have forgotten the route?

Like a master chess player
he scratches his head
I take this as a sign
he needs to be fed.

His feeds last longer
than a marathon runner,
its the middle of winter
but he's sweating like it's summer.

The milk has made him tipsy
this is my moment to strike
I hold him close to my chest
like a rapper holding a mic.

We gum boot dance around the bedroom
he holds on for dear life
"His eyes are closing"
Words of encouragement from my wife.

He sways like a punch-drunk boxer
making good use of the ropes
I try to counter his jabs
by singing Caribbean lullaby notes.

"Yellow bird
Up high in banana tree"

His response,

"I am the greatest
I float like a butterfly
And sting like a bee"

Ding Ding!
12th and final round
One of us will remain standing
the other is going down.

We enter a clinch
for the very last time
I unleash a deadly combination
of dance and rhyme.

Every step I take
I recite another line
he's dazed and confused
he's out on his feet.

One hour and fifty-two minutes later
the warrior concedes defeat
lays down his sword and shield
and boards the train of sleep.

The Drum

The drum is organic like mother's milk,
like a whispered lullaby the drum has sung
loudly unashamedly speaking of times gone by
and times to come.

Bombarding my wall of pretence
like popcorn head butting the pan.
Dissolving my mask like aspirin in water
expression floods my creativity dam.

Ambushed by the rhythm
I surrender autopilot takes control
syllables of sound send Morse code vibrations
to my hungry soul.

I dance like a butterfly, creating 3D images
on the canvas of life with my oil painted feet.
Only the dead remain still
when the Djembe speaks.

We Just A Come

We Just a Come
Yes we just a come
Like the rivers, trees and just like the Sun.

Each and every morning the sun rises at dawn
And each and every day another baby is born.
Look at the sea how it keeps on turning
just like the sea you got to keep on learning.
Step by step the tree of life you should be climbing
Let your light shine bright never let it go dim
though the river is deep don't be afraid to swim.

We Just a Come
Yes we just a come
Like the rivers, trees and just like the Sun.

It takes many rivers to form the ocean
All types of people to build a nation
It takes many branches to make one Tree
It takes a mother and a father to raise a family
Both need foundation and roots are the keys
Without roots you'll be swept away by the Sea.

We Just a Come
Yes we just a come
Like the rivers, trees and just like the Sun.

Unstoppable, incredible we're still moving on
against all odds maybe a billion to one.
Driven by the energy we get from the Sun
From the tree of life we took the wood to make a drum
Winter turns to spring and seconds embrace the hours
Now you can't force the bud into a flower
And if the water doesn't run it must turn sour.

We Just a Come
Yes we just a come
Like the rivers, trees and just like the Sun.

The Sun rises and the Sun must fall
now this is a message, a message to all.
Notice how the tree stands proud and tall
try to know yourself before your back's against the wall.
Yes we've come a long way, but the road is still long
as we rise to the challenge we will all sing this song.

We Just a Come
Yes we just a come
Like the rivers, trees and just like the Sun.

Tardis of Culture

Ridley market sends her love
for she could not be here in person.

Let's paint blue notes on this concrete canvas
watch chaos reform as abstract art.
Let's re-assemble this human jigsaw
in Hackney's opera we all play a part.

On this marble chessboard we are kings
in this geographical equation N16 Ö = 1
space nurtures her daughter reflection
who gives birth to reasoning her son.

Who needs Bluetooth or wi-fi?
When we have palm trees and jazz.

Take off your shoes
step inside this Tardis of culture
leave all baggage by the blue door.
The country comes to Dalston
as we square dance beneath U.F.O. lights
on this tarmac ballroom floor.

Old man time runs out of breath
and slumps on a bench to catch the view.
It's a twilight zone experience,
something so ancient appears so new.

Listen to the global village orchestra
indulge in the language buffet
drink from the well of understanding
let's re-write the history books today.

We'll pour libation by the roadside
ocean traffic laps against the Rio shore.
We'll square the circle to the drumbeat
then ngoma till our feet are sore

This cosmopolitan island,
overlooking the Kingsland stream
welcomes all partner-ships
to dock in Gillett harbour
and manifest their dreams.

Embrace your birthright
this A10 amphitheatre bears your name.
Walk barefoot on wet cement
on the Gillett boulevard walk of fame.

Wear it with pride

Some wear it like a badge of honour
others hide it like a scar.
Some are inspired by countries
a few by flashy motorcars.

Some shorten theirs
to be cool and part of the crowd.
Some have silent letters
while others are rock concert loud.

Some are double-barrel
with hyphens as stubborn as a mule.
There are those that speak of wisdom
while others celebrate the fool.

Some tell of the day you were born
or the order in which you came.
Some speak of humility and grace
whilst others converse on the subject of fame.

Some have tittles before
others sport letters at the end.
Some are universal
they can be worn by women and men.

Some are difficult to pronounce
if you're not willing to try.
Some lose their flavour like bubblegum gum
others are classic and can't die.

There are those linked to history
heroes and she-roes that have gone before.
Some are banks of knowledge
spiritual wealth for the rich and the poor.

Some reflect the power of god
and the righteous path to walk.
Some dance in the hot spring,
of laughter and candyfloss talk.

But only one is special
to the person who wears the crown.
You become immortal
by the ringing of that noun.

Zion train

POSTA, POSTA, FERRY FERRY,
WAY DOCKS, MTWAPA,
THIS IS THE SOUNDTRACK
OF DOWNTOWN MOMBASA

MATATUS STAMPEDE THROUGH
SWISS CHEESE TARMAC ROADS
THE TOUTS SPEAK IN MATATU CODES
WHIPPING THEIR PUNTERS INTO A FRENZY
LIKE A RAGGA DJ HYPING HIS CROWD
WAILING TO THE PEOPLE
"Get on board the Zion train coming your way"

THE COMPETITION IS FIERCE
WORDS ARE THROWN LIKE SPEARS
AT THE SMILING OPPOSITION
THIS RACE IS FOR THE SWIFT
ONLY THE FITTEST WILL SURVIVE
IT'S 15 KSH FROM KENOL TO POSTA
IF YOU BOARD AT BAMBURI BEACH
THEN, IT'S AN EXTRA FIVE

POSTA, POSTA, FERRY FERRY,
WAY DOCKS, MTWAPA,
THIS IS THE SOUNDTRACK
OF DOWNTOWN MOMBASA

OUR CONDUCTOR IS A FUNDI AT PACKING
WE'RE LAYERED CLOSELY, LIKE PRINGLES IN A TUB
MAKING ROOM OUT OF THE IMPOSSIBLE
A BIT LIKE FORCING EIGHT FINGERS
INTO A FIVE FINGER GLOVE

SPEEDING LIKE A FORMULA 1 CAR
THE DRIVER DOES BATTLE WITH NATURE
AS HE TRY'S TO OVERTAKE THE WIND
LEAPFROGGING OVER POT HOLES,
YOUR STOMACH ENTERS YOUR MOUTH
WE CLING TO OUR SEATS
LIKE A BABY KANGAROO IN ITS MOTHERS POUCH

POSTA, POSTA, FERRY FERRY,
WAY DOCKS, MTWAPA,
THIS IS THE SOUNDTRACK
OF DOWNTOWN MOMBASA

HIP HOP, SOUL AND REGGAE VIBRATIONS
PUNCTURE THE SUNDRENCHED AIR
EVERYBODY LOOKS DRUNK,
AS WE
GOOSE NECK TO THE BASS AND THE DRUM
WE'RE SYNCHRONISED
LIKE OLYMPIC SWIMMERS
FOR A SPLIT MOMENT WE'RE ONE

WE EXIT AT THE ROAD SIDE
A BIG SMILE HIJACKS OUR FACE
FEAR RUSHES LIKE STEAM
FROM OUR BODIES
JOY QUICKLY TAKES ITS PLACE

WE BID THEM FAREWELL (KWEHERI)
AS WE PICK UP OUR LOAD
THE JOY IS SHORT LIVED

FOR NOW
WE HAVE TO CROSS THE ROAD.

(MATATUS = 12 SEATER MINI BUS, THAT MANAGES
TO CARRY 20 PEOPLE
FUNDI = SWAHALI WORD FOR EXPERT)

A Love Poem

I be the sun who rises
And penetrates your earth
You be the fertile soil that nourishes
Until springtime, when you give birth

You be the seductive oil in the lamp
And I be the drunkard wick
You be hands of time in perpetual motion
I be the gearing mechanism to make you tick

I be the silver bullet inside your barrel
You squeeze the trigger for my gun
I be the tall dark sugarcane
You be the grinder that yields the rum

I be the patchwork quilt keeping your heart warm
I be the thread in your needle
Use me to repair it when it's torn

I am the black in your berry
You be the passion in my fruit
I be the yeast in your flour
You be the sprinkle of thyme in my soup

I be your X & Y axis
Etching my soul on your graph
You be the drifting piece of wood
In the ocean of my mind that I use as a raft

I be the pulsating, hypnotic rhythm
You be the toffee flavored morish blues
I be the turntable needle
Spinning at 33rpm
Riding in the valley of your grooves

You be original like a snowflake
Different every time you fall
I be the whisper of the fire
Can't you hear me call?

I be the sixty minutes in your hour
You be the seven sunsets of my week
I be the 359 degrees,
You be the 1 to make our orbit complete
I be the melatonin secretion in the depths of your sleep
You be serotonin feeding my third eye
As the sun reaches its peak

I be the Alpha the beginning
And you be the Omega the end
All of this, and more is possible
Because you are my friend

I am carnival

London is no longer naked
Picasso's brush has kissed human skin.
The world unites on one doorstep
now the masquerade can begin.

 A million voices crescendo
all speaking the same tongue.
The sound system speaker pays respect
to the godfather, the African drum.

A sea of hands holds the heavens aloft
as if offering the creator a prayer.
Baselines embrace slippery waistlines
the rhythm is so moving, even the statues shed a tear.

Sound bites have no place in this parliament
the government has come to the streets.
In this global democracy
the people vote with their feet.

Some bring red, some bring yellow
then fly their flags to salute the day.
The young find wisdom in an elder's face
the old remember the joys of play.

And above the music
we hang our dreams on the shoulders of hope
riding this runaway train
harmonizing on the same note.

Which sounds like

I am London!
I am the World!
I am Carnival!

Poetry Revolution

So it's a poetry revolution
where no one dies
and people stand back and say
"Oh me oh my"
Where drama lives beyond the stage
where the least important thing standing is the mic
where politics and love bleed together on the page
Gather round now
And Listen!
To the story teller
Brappp!
Get down.
This story is live.

Verbalizm

Verbalizm
We hit them with the verbalizm
Verbalizm
We lick them with the verbalizm

From the canvas of chaos
out of the depths of the storm.
From the river of remembrance
Verebalizm is born.

Relentless in its mission
mercy not in its DNA
these fluid larva lyrics
brand the world
Verbalizm is here to stay

Their satellite navigation
cannot track my instrument my pen.
The Verbalizer drops information
faster than CNN.

Verbalizm
We hit them with the verbalizm
Verbalizm
We lick them with the verbalizm

A voice from the voiceless
a light house in the dark
words dance to the music
organic rhythms from the heart.

This blockbuster movie
has no beginning
until you create the end.

No leading actors
just six billion extras
of women, children and men.

Verbalizm
We hit them with the verbalizm
Verbalizm
We lick them with the Verbalizm

A serial seducer
composing mango chords.
This surgical script
cuts like swords

through the walls of hype
above the clouds of depression
through minefields of denial
severing moments of aggression.

Through dead-ends that lead to somewhere
through the traffic of my mind
through the dreams of tomorrow
to the place where we find

Verbalizm
We hit them with the verbalizm
(Chorus)
Verbalizm
We lick them with the verbalizm.

What is music?

What's this thing called music?
And what's it for?
Music was made for dancing!
Are you sure?

Many times I listen
a few times I hear.
Some times I shy away like a kid
drunk on the wine of fear.

Muddy baselines take me down
to the place I call home.
There's no one here
But I swear I'm not alone.

I'm sitting comfortably
I have no need for a chair
I start to drown
but there's no water
I'm breathing music
like it was air.

Music takes me to the bridge
JB Style.
I'm rude boy stepping on my six string bow
I try to rest but I know it's time to go.

Bob was right
when music hits you,
you feel no pain.
Man it knocked me out!

Revived by the snare drum
beating down like rain.
Blood surges like electricity
through my trombone veins.

Walking words
hands on double bass.
Smoothing out the creases
in history's face.

So hit the symbols of chaos
blow the saxophones of flight.
Roll the drumsticks of resistance
let the trumpets impregnate the night.

Let the Be-bop
groove with Hip-Hop
Let Rag-time jam with Ragga

Let the blues gyrate to Soca
As you climb this Lip-hop ladder.

Caboodle Books proudly presents

Lip Hopping with the Fundi-Fu,

performance poetry by

Adisa The Verbalizer.

This collection of poetry captures some of Adisa's most celebrated
poems that have thrilled and inspired school audiences
from London to Zimbabwe.

To order your copies please complete the form and return it with a
cheque made payable to Caboodle Books Limited.

Name/School/Organization...

Address ....

....

....

Copies required............................

Price: £5.99 (£1.00 postage)

Total ....

Send form and payment to : Caboodle Books Ltd.
Riversdale, 8 Rivock Avenue, Steeton, BD20 6SA.